I0088520

A Girl's
GOTTA HAVE HER OWN
Money!

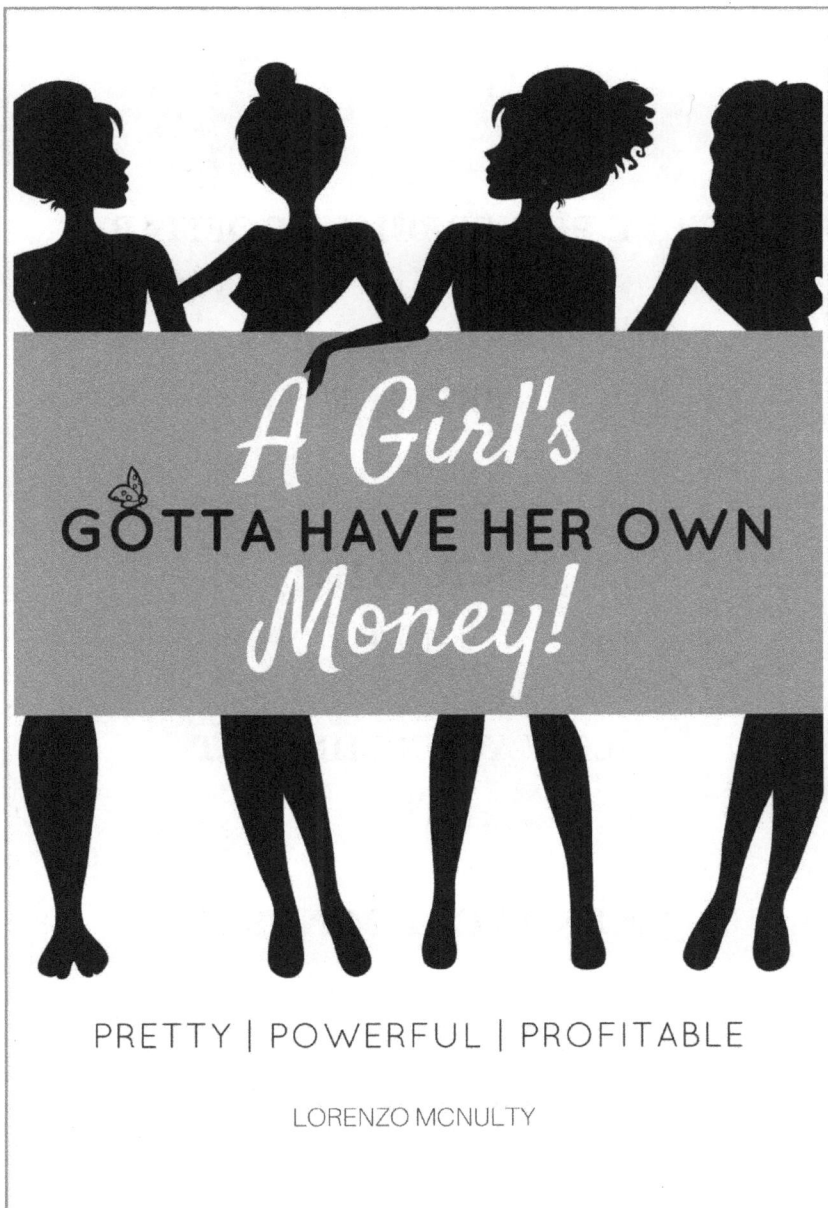

PRETTY | POWERFUL | PROFITABLE

LORENZO MCNULTY

CONTENTS

CONTENTS

PRETTY | POWERFUL | PROFITABLE

A letter to you, my loves.

This story is dedicated to the most beautiful people in my life; my wife, Ma (mom) and daughters. You ladies are my reason. There are many things said that a man should do in this world. I have found that of those things, the most important is to take care of our girls. The principles I'll share here are of you , by you, and for you - my girls. Thank you and I love you.

This book is also dedicated to my own father and each father alike. If you take nothing from me ever again, take and carry with you my belief in building up our girls to the tremendously influential people they were put on this earth to be.

My grandmother once told me about the relationship between the gardener and his fields. How he is given his field to tend, to seed, and to protect from those things out to harm it. She also taught me to celebrate its harvest and how to be thankful for each sprout. We are the gardeners and our girls are our fields. Tend to them with care and they will produce well beyond our greatest hopes for them.

Though this message is directed at ladies, the principles shared can and should be used by parents for both girls and boys to grow them into successful, strong upholders of their own truths.

PREFACE

My brother was on the other line and I could already tell he was in tears. I knew something was wrong and was instantly on alert because my brother never cries. I asked in our common phrase every time we greet each other on the phone. "Aye, what up, man?" I asked in an attempt to bring normalcy to the conversation. He said two words that would immediately impact the entire trajectory of my life.. and his.

It was colder than usual on this night in Hattiesburg, Mississippi. I was late closing down my store after a busier day than we had seemingly had in awhile. I was tired but feeling accomplished. I had just set the alarm and was headed toward the door as my phone rang. It was normal for me to get phone calls, yet the timing and the feeling in the air made this one different somehow.

"Don died," he said.

I felt the air get too heavy to inhale. It was not as cold anymore. I could feel my thoughts frantically rushing to find the response that could solve the problem I knew could not be solved. It hurt and the only response I could offer after what felt like an eternity was, "where's Ma?"

He went on to explain that Don had been rushed to the hospital in Jackson, Mississippi where he was pronounced dead after a massive heart-attack. It felt as if I was hanging onto each word as to dissect it into something more believable. I did not want to believe what he was saying was true. I could not accept it. Don was the only father I knew. Sure my grandfather was awesome and uncles were all truly great in teaching me many things; Don was the person who showed me what being a man in a house was supposed to look like. I always thought it weird how the level of appreciation and respect we have for people changes when we can no longer show that respect and appreciation.

As humans, we seemingly appreciate tombstones more than the people beneath them. I am no different. I immediately thought of all the knowledge he gave me freely. I thought of all the ways I behaved because he wasn't my biological father. I encourage you to not learn this lesson the hard way as I did.

These moment's are far too precious and that increased vision that comes with hindsight often lets us see a very real truth about ourselves.

The hospital was a 2-hour drive from Hattiesburg to Jackson. It was one of the darkest, quietest rides of my life. I kept seeing flashes of instances where I could have been better. I saw times where we were all laughing and happy. I then saw my mom. My mom was now tasked with finding a way to push forward after losing her closest friend, her partner, her husband.

As I got closer to the hospital and saw it glowing in the dark form all its lights, I thought of how my mom would now be faced with the bills - only, this time alone. Without half of her household income, how would she do it?

"Epiphanies are like rainbows. They are often boldest after storms."

Unknown

KNOW YOUR "WHY"

Find your "why"; Find your way.

For my readers, especially if you're in the course for this book currently; I have two daughters, sometimes three depending on the mood my wife is in (joking.. love you). My oldest lives primarily with her mom in Mississippi. My youngest daughter, who we call Bug, lives with us in North Carolina. She's a tremendous kid. Beautiful, brilliant, and what some would call bossy. We call that leadership in our house. Another side of this story would tell you how we went from being pregnant wit her in a one bedroom apartment on the 3rd floor to the home we have now.

This story is about her impact on my view of women and finances. Michelle always tells her the importance of a girl having her own money. I'm unsure if she knew of the seed she was sewing into my heart at the time. I thank her for it nonetheless.

I thought of the immediate shift in my mom's financial situation with the loss of her spouse. I thought of how my wife would handle it should she have to face losing my portion of the household income. I think of my daughters being in this situation. I spoke of my granny earlier and her wisdom regarding the care of our fields. I now know to teach my children about financial fitness, especially my girls. Here are a few shocking statistics as to why:

Women earned 78.3 cents for every dollar men earned in 2014
- *The Wallstreet Journal*

3 of 5 women over 65 cannot afford to cover their basic needs.

Marriage eases the financial burden, but most women outlive their male partners. 2/3 of men over 65 live with a partner, while less than half (44%) of women over 65 live with a partner.

The number of older women living in poverty is 50% higher than older men living in poverty.
- *Analysis of U.S. Census data by Wider Opportunities for Women*

About 20 to 30 years are spent in retirement, and experts suggest you have at least 70 to 90 percent of your pre-retirement income saved for each retirement year to continue your current lifestyle. Women, however, need 100 percent to make up for
lower pay, years out of the workforce, and longer lifespan.
 - *What Women Need to Know About Retirement: A joint project of the Heinz Family Philanthropies and the Women's Institute for a Secure Retirement. (http:// www.heinzfamily.org/ebook/ebook.pdf)*

I know that with purpose, I can impact my girls' positions here. This is why I began to study the habits of millionaires. Lots and lots of them. It's funny and ironic that the ones most easily found were men. I'll tell you here what we tell our daughters every opportunity we have: "girls can do anything boys can do." We are raising Chief Executive Officers (CEOs), capable of taking on any challenge with the decisiveness and intelligence to come out as a success in the topics that matter. I am teaching them to understand that they are a business and how to operate as one when needed. Here, I offer that to you.

This book is written for the amazing women our girls will grow to be. Its purpose is to inspire them to not only face the barriers of gender, but to break through them sooner and with purpose. I believe that every girl has something amazing to offer this world, and this is written to aid those who believe the same in securing a position of stability in their future. It is written as coursework due to the intentionality that coursework requires.

Understand that your finances should be treated no differently. Should you desire to see increase in any aspect of your life, begin to do these simple things immediately.

Be purposeful with your reading these following pages so that you may grasp the concepts shared by millionaires to a degree in which you can take them and teach them to your girls. I encourage you to highlight and scribble notes throughout of what inspires you, and pass this gift to your own girls. The best way to retain and reinforce what you have learned is to teach another. At the end of each module you will find a page for notes. It's important to write down your ideas. Everyone grab a partner!

I will show you how to become the LEADER of your life by assuming the role of CEO of your Family, Finances and your Business. Accept this promotion. You absolutely deserve it. As we grow through this book, I will introduce terms to you that will be helpful in this book as well as once you begin to complete the coursework.

It is important to also note that what you read here cannot be unlearned. You will begin to see your world differently as it relates to growing and increasing your wealth potential. Things you have seen each and everyday will begin to reveal a different meaning. You will be financially educated. Embrace it. You were put here to be profitable.

"The best protection any woman can have ... is courage."

Elizabeth Cady Stanton

(1815–1902), US social reformer. With Lucretia Mott, she organized the first US women's rights convention, in Seneca Falls, New York, in 1848. From 1852, she led the women's rights movement with Susan B. Anthony.

Create Notes:

_____

_____

_____

_____

_____

_____

_____

_____

_____

_____

_____

_____

_____

_____

_____

BLOW YOUR MINDSET
Perception IS Reality

First and foremost - Forget what you think you know about money. To live in abundance we have to relearn the concept of what money's PURPOSE is and why it's important. Robert Kiyosaki once said, "It's not how much money you make, but how much money you keep, how hard IT WORKS FOR YOU, and how many generations you keep it for." Once I began to understand that, my life began to shift from Ramen noodles to noodles from Rome, and yours can too with the really easy tips I'll share with you in this book.

From this moment forward, money = "WEALTH". Refer to it as such in your conversations moving forward. We look at people with money different than people with wealth. It is simply due to the fact that we have been conditioned to think this way. Here's an exercise:

Close your eyes and imagine what "money" looks like. Got it? Now, close your eyes and think of what "wealth" looks like. You likely saw cash in one instance and another form of CAPITAL in the other. I'll let you play with that one. This is a great exercise to use in your own financial classes for engagement purposes.

CAPITAL is wealth available in the form of money or other assets OWNED by a person or organization.

Note to Remember: There is approximately $1.39 trillion in circulation as of September 30, 2015. There were 319 million people in the U.S. in 2014. That is enough to put a cash amount of $4300 in every man, woman, and child's pocket in the entire United States. Don't shortchange yourself because you believe there's not enough wealth in this world. There is an ABUNDANCE. You just gotta think bigger!

There was a time where I thought having more wealth was in bad taste and that the wealthy were just plain old bad people for stepping on the backs of others to reach a dollar. As a result of this thinking, I subconsciously aligned "being HUMBLE" with "staying BROKE". Being humble does NOT equal staying broke. If you currently are where I was then.. Get out of the scarcity mentality! I did not want people to think that I had forgotten where I came from. I wanted to "keep it real". I was wrong. That is the harsh reality that a little boy from the housing projects of Mississippi had to struggle to learn. I had a terrible case of the scarcity MINDSET and it was pinning me to the ground without me even recognizing it.

Here's the truth about a position of wealth. Wealthy is POWERFUL. That's it. The end. You control your ability to receive it and equally important, you control where it is transferred. Before we get too deeply into wealth transferral, lets talk about a few tips to crush that scarcity mindset and better position you to receive the wealth you DESIRE. The benefits you will gain from this transition of mindset are worth more than gold! You will be wealthier, wiser, and happier. Who doesn't want those things in their life today? *To defeat an enemy, we must first know and understand how to IDENTIFY it*. Here is what the scarcity mindset does to you subconsciously:

It forces you to spend all you have while you have it so that it cannot be taken away from you. This puts you into the paycheck-to-paycheck CYCLE. This is where we are being paid every 2 weeks and manage our money poorly enough to last for 11 of the 14 days, or when we are paid monthly and things consistently begin to get a little tight at day 25 of 30. The scarcity mentality/mindset is why this happens to you. It ignores the bigger picture and forces you into extremely short-termed decision-making. This pushes you into a never ending cycle of fixing issues that you create yourself. It creates more work for no reward.

It breeds jealousy, and jealousy creates sadness. Ever had those thoughts where you think that what you have is less VALUABLE than what another has? I have. I was sad because of the value I placed on something I did not have. Here's a secret: Value is perceived which means it is CONTROLLABLE.

"To attract money, you must focus on wealth. It's impossible to bring more money into your life when you are noticing you don't have enough, because that means you are thinking thoughts that you do not have enough. Focus on not enough money, and you will create untold more circumstances of not having enough money. You must focus on the abundance of money to bring that to you."

Rhonda Byrne

Rhonda Byrne is best known for her 2006 self-help book, "The Secret," based on how the power of positive thinking can create wealth and happiness. By 2007, "The Secret" had sold more than 19 million copies in over 40 languages (more than two million DVDs were also sold), grossing over $300 million dollars including profits from the film by the same name. Really good reading!

Create Notes:

_____

_____

_____

_____

_____

_____

_____

_____

_____

_____

MEND YOUR MINDSET
Embrace a New Way of Thinking

The following is a secret that every multi-MILLIONAIRE knows well and exercises on purpose. In every avenue of our life, we must understand that we ATTRACT what we believe in. ← Say this out loud right now. Take care in your thoughts. If they go off course, pause, then realign them with positive PURPOSE. There is no better time than now to revisit your goal out loud and in writing. A great example of this is in a book by Napoleon Hill called *Think and Grow Rich*. It talks about the power of PERSISTENT thought and transforming your thoughts into the tangible.

One of the most easily overlooked and most powerful impacts on what we think and believe is our environment and who we spend our time with. Be attentive to your

ATMOSPHERE. There is a saying about birds and feathers that will once again prove useful here. It is true.

In writing this, I desperately searched to find the author of this quote in order to give due credit. The quotes says, "show me your FRIENDS and I'll show you your FUTURE."

I found myself in a really tough situation at the end of 2014 largely due to the surroundings I chose but primarily due to my subsequent decisions. I know the POWER of our atmosphere first hand and am constantly planting this seed with my girls to help them grow from my mistakes. Mending a MINDSET sometimes takes some assistance. Surround yourself with life-breathing, uplifting, positive people. Make sure these people have goals and ambitions equal to or greater than your own. Their very presence will instantly push you into a space of creativity and desire for MAGNIFICENT things from this world. Things that will take effort, but things that you definitely deserve.

The last secret to mending your mindset is another SHIFT. I know. I know. I'm asking a lot and if you've

gotten this far, this next secret is going to change everything you know. It is the mentality I embraced that took me from a $14.12 check to over 6 figures and counting. I now understand how it is THE most critical step in mending your MINDSET and it has yielded me an immeasurable amount of happiness. There is no one word to describe it in its sheer magnitude, so I will do my best to express it in two segments.

TRANSITION your mind from spending to investing. ← Say this out loud right now. From now forward, do your best to eliminate the thought of "SPENDING". Once you get deeper into this book, you will uncover secrets to unlock wealth in your life. That will not be enough. To maintain the wealth by making it create wealth is the job of a CEO. Now do you understand where I am going with the promotion you deserve? This is what you will be tasked with. You will have to make sure you are making the moves to make the kingdom more magnificent in your LEGACY.

I will make it easy for you by explaining the transition from spending to investing, but first do you know the difference? I did not at first. I now know that the difference in spending and INVESTING is that only one of the two yields dividends. When you spend, it's simply spent and you move on with the loss. *When you invest, you expect DIVIDENDS*. To break this down further let me explain my recent experiment.

I had my eyes on these Balmain Biker jeans (in black). I wanted these jeans and when I say I wanted these jeans - I. Wanted. These. Jeans. On sale, they were about $1300. the price coupled with my tendency to RESEARCH everything made me wait. As I waited the decision began to gain more OBJECTIVITY than the SUBJECTIVITY that I was already experiencing. Here's a freebie: Give yourself time to objectify your decision on anything major.

This allows you to create a space to make DECISIONS that aren't primarily based on emotion or subjective to the circumstances you feel.

Instead of purchasing those jeans, I purchased a Certificate of DEPOSIT (CD) that you can find at most any bank along with other high-yield savings vehicles. This will get really fun when we talk about *CDs* later. That was at the beginning of January. I deposited an additional $100 each month since. At the end of this year, I will have CREATED $17.64 out of thin air. Although those jeans would have made me look dope, they would not have grown wealth for me by owning them. I know that in order to ensure my girls know how to keep themselves dope looking but with bank accounts to match.

Far too many want to look more valuable than they are. I encourage you in the other direction. Be more VALUABLE than what you look. They must know how to invest.

As you are reading this, *the greatest investment in your future is an investment in yourself*. Never doubt that. Investing does not stop there. The investment of TIME is much greater. Time is an ever-depleting resource. It is tricky due to us being incapable of putting a number to it in regards to how much we have left. Be sure you are investing your time whenever you can. There is something about it that ENHANCES life in a way that nothing else can. Investing time in my relationship with my wife was like covering it in magic fairy dust.

First, I had to recognize where I was wasting time, then reallocate that time to something that would PRODUCE better fruits of my labor. It enhanced our relationship, our parenting, our individual growth and our professional growth. In order to not turn this into a relationship book, I'll just ask that you invest your time into things that will give you a return on your investment. Ok ladies, lets get into the fun stuff about wealth building and management!

I would encourage you to reread this paragraph as EVERYTHING begins and end with your perception of your own wealth and the mindset you embrace moving forward.

"The greatest discovery of all time is that a person can change his future by merely changing his attitude."

Oprah Winfrey

Oprah Winfrey is a US television talk-show host, actress, producer, and philanthropist. In 1984, she started as a talk-show host on A.M. Chicago, which evolved into the nationally televised Oprah Winfrey Show (1986–2011).

Create Notes:

_____

_____

_____

_____

_____

_____

_____

_____

_____

_____

_____

_____

THE 'CEO' APPROACH

Creating a Space for Better Decisions

Now that we have blown and mended our mindset. Let us unpack the idea of The CEO Approach. The CEO MINDSET is all about making decisions in the toughest areas for the greater good of the empire (I.e., the relationship with your spouse, your kids, your business, etc.) At my day job, I get to teach people how to embrace a moment of objectivity in order to help them to see the bigger picture. It is called Critical THINKING. It is a highly sought after skill and many do not have it so those of us that do - get paid. First, you must ask yourself what's most important. Whatever that is, align all your ENERGY in that direction and be unwavering in pursuit of it.

Before I began writing this book course, I spoke with Michelle in depth about her financial beliefs.

I wanted to make sure that we were on the same map, in the same DIRECTION heading towards the same destination. Let me pause here and say that if you are in a committed relationship as you are reading this, pay close attention to the next few lines. They could make or break the EMPIRE you are working so hard to build.

I was recently on a call where I was asked about the bank accounts of people in relationships and if they should share them or not. I took the CEO approach to making that call. The approach makes you align all of your decisions with that of a business. The CEO's best interest is in the flourishing of the business (i.e., the home, the relationship, etc.). With that, I say that all the funds go to the company and the employees are paid a salary. What that means is that the household income should pay the regular operating expenses and each CEO should receive their payment from that. You have to pay the people who make the company work.

Before you dig into all of that, you must make sure all personnel are on the same page. Have an open discussion about your financial position and your plans moving FORWARD. Both of you are required to behave as CEOs if you want that empire. This means having uncomfortable conversations for the betterment of that empire. This also means coming together and MAPPING out a plan for the future. Because of it's foundational importance, I have included a GUIDE to make it easier a little for you.

"It is very important to know who you are. To make decisions. To show who you are."

Malala Yousafzai

Malala Yousafzai is a Pakistani activist for female education and the youngest-ever Nobel Prize laureate.

She is known mainly for human rights advocacy for education and for women in her native Swat Valley in the Khyber Pakhtunkhwa province of northwest Pakistan, where the local Taliban had at times banned girls from attending school. Yousafzai's advocacy has since grown into an international movement. Her family runs a chain of schools in the region.

Start the Finance conversation without sounding like a jerk.

The purpose of this conversation is to get both of you looking at the same map going in the same direction to the same destination, financially.

The Approach to a conversation is equally, if not more important than the body of the conversation. It's the door you have to enter and your approach can determine if you are welcomed in, or stumbling backwards from having said door slammed in your face. Here are 2 tried and true approaches that will work on almost anyone.

The Hypothetical Approach:
If you inherited $XX,XXX.00, what would you invest it in?

I like this approach because it is not pointed and does what judges call "leading the witness". You get your counterpart into the mind frame you need them to be in by asking a non threatening questions but planting the thought of investing and finances.

The Direct Approach:

I've been thinking a lot about investing lately. You know anything that would help?

This approach is great because it's not only non-threatening, it demands engagement without demanding engagement. Aside from that, everyone likes to help the ones they love.

You have the conversation started. Now what?? Keeping the end-goal in mind, the **Topics** you talk to are the support to your approach. *You can lead a horse to water, but you can't make him drink*. Every heard this idiom? Do you know why the horse doesn't drink? It's simply because the more is not convinced that he is thirsty.

There is no value in drinking the water for him. He's not "bought-in". As humans, we need to hear a WIFM, a what's in it for me BEFORE we go along with the plan. The topics you choose should create that "*I win*" feeling for the other person. In the spirit of making it a breeze for you, below are 3 easy intros that are all but money in the bag.

Topics:

Saving - Easy Starter.
"How much do you try to put away each year/month/pay cycle?"
"Have you found any good savings vehicles?"

Budgeting - Moderate Starter.
"I'm really trying to find a good method for budgeting."
"I'm challenged with my budget, because...."

Future - Moderate to Difficult Starter.
"What do you think about going to Paris next summer?"

"Xxxxx is retiring soon and it got me to thinking about our retirement plans."

During my tenure as leaders in both the Marine Corps and in the corporate world, I have learned that there are 3 things that have accomplished more goals than Neiman Marcus has shoes. Committing to your vision, following up on your vision, and having fun while you do it. Thats it.

Commitment speaks for itself. When you commit to a goal you inherently say, "There is no going back: I must finish what I started." All YOU have to do is .. do what you said you would do.

Once you've committed, set a cycle for **Follow-up**. As a CEO, your ability to follow up is key to your successful completion of goals.

It is a method of mitigating / lessening the impact of failure. How would you feel knowing that failure would feel a little less painful as you got closer and closer to achieving your goal?

What would you do with that power?

Lastly, make it interesting and **Make It Fun**. Too many people get old and regret not enjoying the food when they had the teeth to chew it. Enjoy this journey. Smile 'til it hurts and laugh yourself into tears. Here are 3 Secrets to make your goal work:

Closing Commitments:
AGREE on the steps you are going to take to accomplish your goals and write them down. Writing your goals down is the first way to make them tangible. Create a schedule of when the investment will happen. Highlight where you are today to use as a reference point for success later.

Follow-up:

This step is critical to the success of any and every CEO. We must inspect what we expect. Create check points to sit down and review where you are in relation to where you started.

I would recommend the follow up occurring on the month's end as dividends are normally deposited then.

Make It Fun!

Create a chart where you can track and celebrate your increases. Create a vision board of things you will do once you've accomplished your goal. There are tons of great ideas out there to help keep your vision in front of you.

Create Notes:

_____

_____

_____

_____

_____

_____

_____

_____

_____

_____

_____

_____

_____

VISIONS OF VIRTUE
Your Level of Persistence is Inspired By Your 'Why'

If you have read this far, you deserve the SECRETS I am going to share with you, however, I want to let you know how very real and significant these things are to me and the life of my girls. Notice that I have not mentioned that I am some sort of financial guru or genius of any sort. I am simply a man with a VISION for the future of his family, his field as my granny would call it. The things I am sharing with you have been learned through tremendous pain and through which, a discovery of a strength I did not know was available to me. I have failed over and over again. I have been broke and broken and that created the PASSION with which I greet you today. You are the first to ever read this story as I have never shared it out loud with anyone else.

I remember the days of living in the government housing well, however those days are not as clear of a reminder as what I am about to SHARE with you. It was late August, 2009. If you have ever visited North Carolina, you know how sweltering the humid air can be during the late summer. We were newlyweds; young, HAPPY, poor and pregnant. We lived in a tiny one bedroom apartment that rested at the top of three flights of wooden stairs.

We both worked part-time jobs. I attended school in the morning and went from there straight to WORK at night. Retail hours were an absolute strain on our relationship, but we needed the lights and the Vienna-fried rice we seemed to live on at the time. If you are not familiar with Vienna sausages, I ENCOURAGE you to look it up for better imagery. We owned a bed and all borrowed furniture. There was a point where we were selling our clothes to make and end meet. I still had the scarcity MENTALITY and that made me comfortable with the struggle to make ends meet. Michelle was now entering her 8th month of pregnancy.

Pregnant with a baby that would come into this world weighing more than, she did the grocery shopping while I was at work, and had to carry them up those three flights of wooden stairs. I came home one day, tired and STRESSED and saw her crying. I asked what was wrong and the words she said to me changed something within me that has been forever changed since. Through her tears, she said, "I don't want to be 9 months pregnant and climbing those stairs." That moment in that summer CHANGED our lives.

The PRESSURE to provide a place for my wife and child were growing quickly, and the bills were seemingly endless. I needed to make a terribly hard decision. I knew my mom wanted me to finish school and I knew I could not have my Bug coming home to that apartment. To me the DECISION was obvious - I quit school. My focused switched to my career in sales to build more wealth but more importantly, I began to pour into the vision I had that night. I saw her bringing Bug home to her OWN house with her own room with her own bed.

With no knowledge on home buying, I spent the next 3 weeks researching, RELENTLESSLY. I was up at 3 and 4am on our desktop computer looking up neighborhoods, houses, and crime reports. There were many nights I did not go to sleep and the days and nights seemed to string together as one. I made a promise to her, and that little girl on the way, that I would GIVE this world every ounce of me to ensure they never had to suffer this way again. Ever.

During this period of time I was forced to review every penny we owned for COSTS we were not even aware existed. *It taught me to watch my money and forced me into a space were I had to let it sit. Untouched. Unspent.* It taught me to get to know money. We closed on our new home that same month, just in time for Bug to arrive mid-September.

There is a LESSON in persistence here, but that is not what this story is about. I learned the secret to wealth, and it was in the fruit of a vision.

There will be many people and things along your JOURNEY into your purpose and vision that will want nothing more from you than pull you off the path to enjoy their idea of comfort. Some will be for good reason, and some will be so that you do not SURPASS them. Understand these two things: Comfort comes at the cost of your growth, and your vision will create discomfort when it senses that you are not giving it the attention it requires.

That gut feeling that we often wish we had listened to is our PURPOSE screaming from within us. Rest, yet understand that your vision needs you to get back to the path.

"When I dare to be powerful, to use my strength in the service of my vision, then it becomes less and less important whether I am afraid."

Audre Lorde

Andre Lorde was a Caribbean-American writer, radical feminist, womanist, lesbian, and civil rights activist. In her own words, Lorde was a "black, lesbian, mother, warrior, poet". One of her most notable efforts was her activist work with Afro-German women in the 1980s. She spoke on issues surrounding civil rights, feminism, and oppression. Her work gained both wide acclaim and wide criticism, due to the elements of social liberalism and sexuality presented in her work and her emphasis on revolution and change. She died of breast cancer in 1992, at the age of 58.

Create Notes:

_____

_____

_____

_____

_____

_____

_____

_____

_____

_____

_____

KNOW YOUR MONEY
Keep Your Eyes On The Prize!

As a man, I write this with an acute understanding of the male PRIVILEGE that comes with an inherent expectation that we know the money within our home. However, as a man with girls, I have been placed in a uniquely perfect position to break that cycle. We are growing CEOs. They will make executive, INTELLIGENT decisions regarding themselves and their financials.

Today Michelle posted a quote from a lady who wrote a women's empowerment book. It said something to the point of women should not wait on anyone to be there to take care of her. I agree with her and would add that women should be breaking that narrative to its knees. *It's okay to own your own.* GROW yourself. In the next couple pages, I will tell you the secrets to doing just that.

With that, the greatest piece of understanding that I can give my girls in regards to building WEALTH and experiencing an abundance in the financial area of their life is the understanding of the cash flow PRINCIPLE. Cash Flow is the money being transferred into and out of the business, especially impacting liquidity. This refers to the money going in and out of your pocket.

Cash flow requires your attention to prevent the shock of being broke "before you know it". KNOW your money. I know we've all had that moment where we have enough money for the next 3 days, but payday is 5 - 7 days out. If that's just me, I'll own that experience because it taught me something. Being broke for any amount of time stinks. I was speaking to a lady and asking for her feedback on her challenges with creating and GROWING wealth.

We eventually got pretty candid and ended up discussing the frustrations that come from not having access to

WEALTH. There was one particular part of the conversation where she referred to standing in line, frustrated as she checked her bank ACCOUNT. She was frustrated because first, she was having to do it to verify if she had enough money to cover the cost, but second, because the phone service seemed agonizingly slow.

That feeling is called being stuck, and that feeling is never more present than when you have no wealth to MOVE on. Think about the time you wanted a new car or repairs, but simply did not have the resources. Maybe you wanted to move, but your lack of FUNDS created a trap for you. Or maybe it was that piece of clothing that you felt would have taken you from fly to absolutely stunning, but .. you did not have enough purchasing power in the pocket book.

Understanding where your wealth is going can be challenging. Not for the reason most think, but because we have to make ourselves vulnerable to UNDERSTAND it. It hurts to realize you've spent $300+

on eating out and its only been a week. As a coffee snob, I experienced this with my own cash flowing into my favorite coffee shop. I looked at my books and found that I had already spent $75 in a BUSINESS week on Café Marcotters (pronounced *calf-eh mar-ko-tays*) and Palmier cookies. That hurt to see and I needed to own it in order to change it and grow from it.

I want you to COMPLETE this simple activity. It is important as you move through thing book to have created a baseline of cash flow. It is not a budget, so please APPROACH it without the same bore of the chore mentality as we like to do when it comes to budgeting. The simplest of cash flow sheets have a way of encouraging us to modify our behaviors anyway.

"Women have to work much harder to make it in this world. It really pisses me off that women don't get the same opportunities as men do, or money for that matter. Because lets face it, money gives men the power to run the show."

Beyoncé

Beyoncé is an American singer-songwriter, and actress. Born and raised in Houston, Texas, she performed in various singing and dancing competitions as a child, and rose to fame in the late 1990s as lead singer of R&B girl-group Destiny's Child. Managed by her father Mathew Knowles, the group became one of the world's best-selling girl groups of all time. Beyoncé's debut album, Dangerously in Love (2003), sold 12 million copies, earned five Grammy Awards.

HOW TO USE: Enter your total monthly CASH INFLOW in the Right column out from "Deposit". The sheet will allocate budgets for each subsequent category on its own.

This page is intentionally left blank.

CASH FLOW SHEET

ITEM	DATE	INFLOW	OUTFLOW	NET
Beginning Balance	Jan 1	$1127.00		$1127.00
Coffee Shop	Jan 2		$11.00	$1116.00
Bill Payment	Jan 3		$150.00	$966.00
Music (Album)	Jan 4		$11.99	$954.01
Child Care	Jan 6		$150.00	$804.01
Car note	Jan 7		$327.00	$477.01
Cash for Service	Jan 8	$447.00		$477.01
Payday	Jan 9	$1297.00		$477.01
Savings/ Investments	Jan 10		$230.00	$247.01
Business Expense	Jan 10		$90.00	$157.01
Gym Membership	Jan 11		$25.00	$132.01
NET Balance				$132.01

Create Notes:

_____

_____

_____

_____

_____

_____

_____

_____

_____

_____

_____

_____

_____

WEALTH ALLOCATION

Divide and Conquer Being Broke!

You will notice an arrow ➤ highlighting the *Savings/Investments* and the *Business Expenses* rows. I am happy you noticed that was for you. For an ENTREPRENEUR and business owner, these can become blurred lines but need to be separated. I will tell you why not having them can dry up your CASH flow. We will get into that right after we grow through the next topic. Before we dig into the makeup of the savings, we must master *Wealth Allocation*.

When the idea of this book came about, I thought it to be a great idea for me to gather AUTHENTIC feedback from a pretty decent-sized group of women. The conversations were astounding to say the least. The things I learned were shocking at times, yet enlightening all the way. From entrepreneurs, to new moms, to corporate career ladies, to ESTABLISHED women heading into retirement; all had concerns about wealth allocation.

In this section I will tell you about the proven STRATEGY of financial gurus everywhere. We will answer the question of "What wealth goes where and why?" As we grow through this section, keep at the front of your mind that you are the CEO of your life. The best decisions for your future are not always the ones that are most COMFORTABLE for you. As a matter of fact, those decisions are often the least comfortable. Sorry not sorry. That is just the way it is. If anyone suggests any different, they have obviously not run a family or a business.

So what is *wealth allocation*? It is pretty much exactly what it sounds like. You are diving deeper into your cash flow sheet and making it flow to certain areas on purpose. We will use a small corporation as a model for these numbers.

To SIMPLIFY, I'll break it into 4 pieces that can be sliced even thinner depending upon the detail you require. Below displays a simple breakdown of FINANCES to be applied to each cash deposit you receive.

- Operating Costs
- Fun Money
- Charitable Donations
- Savings & Investments

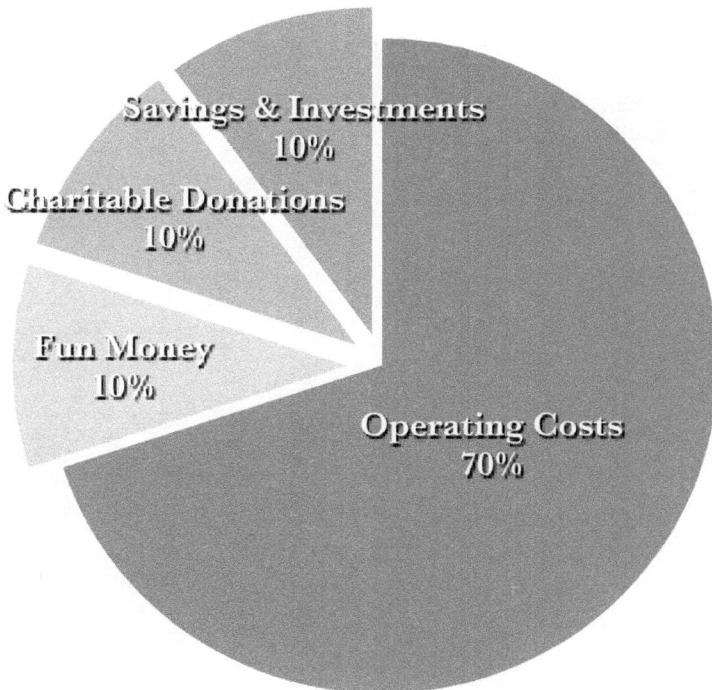

Savings & Investments
10%

Charitable Donations
10%

Fun Money
10%

Operating Costs
70%

HOW TO USE: Enter your Beginning Balance in the gray row. Cash going in your pocket goes in the INFLOW column. Cash going out of your pocket goes in OUTFLOW column.

WEALTH ALLOCATION

CATEGORY	
Deposit (CASH INFLOW)	$7,000.00
Operating Costs	$4,900.00
Savings & Investments	$700.00
Charitable Donation	$700.00
Fun Money	$700.00

Note to Remember: Each item in the category column can be broken into smaller more specified pieces. You can make this as granular as your comfort level allows.

Operating Costs:

The cost required to do BUSINESS on a regular basis is called *Operating Costs*. In companies, it encompasses regularly stocked items, utilities, rent or mortgage. Things that you know will land in your cash OUTFLOW column each week, month, or quarter usually due for payment within a certain timeframe.

Your operating COSTS should be at or less than 70% of your total income for the month. If it is not there presently, do not panic. Later, I will give you a few secrets to bring it back to level. The chart below is plug and play so plug away!

As an entrepreneur, we are subjected to many pitfalls that come in the form of blind spots. I mean, seriously, the word "RISK" is in its definition. We tend to blow money on many schemes and ideas that we don't account for on a regular basis. As an entrepreneur your operating costs should include that $300 you used to have your site built. Include those $10 subscriptions that WORK for you.

The important thing is to track it and make it visible. Do not fall victim to the *gym membership mentality*. This MENTALITY is where you enter a monthly subscription and forget about it as it continuously charges you every month. Is that only me? That's like a slow leak in your car's tire and we all know how that ends.
Patch up those little holes in your INCOME by canceling what you do not use or simply taking the benefit the service offers you and go work out.

Example:

There is a pretty popular gym around our area that charges a monthly fee of $10 for access to their facility. The price is nominal for a reason. That reason is because businesses know that with the million of things we are running around being distracted by, we will forget that $10 being auto-drafted from our account.

One year goes by costing you $120, the second year $240, and so on. Ever purchased something on sale contingent upon a "rebate" that you did not send off by the deadline? Same concept.

Now that company has the legal right to keep that $25 to $100 that enticed you to buy in the first place.

How would it feel to have an additional $240 cash in your pocket right now?

Create Notes:

_____

_____

_____

_____

_____

_____

_____

_____

_____

_____

_____

_____

_____

_____

SAVINGS & INVESTMENTS
Make your money make money!

If I can be TRANSPARENT for another moment; I have gotten the fortune of being able to watch my mom handle her finances. In talking to her, we agree that if we went back we would make different choices. That's a fair statement, right Ma? However, as I watched her, I paid attention to something she did frequently when I was very young. That and losing over $18,000 as a result of a deep lack of financial EDUCATION are things that I attribute many of my own successes to this very day. What I'm about to let you know could potentially blur the line between *Investments* and *Charitable Donations* at first glance. Let me unpack it a bit for deeper understanding of my meaning before you ignore the rest.

First, you will want to grab your **Cash Flow Sheet.**
Second, *begin to mentally transition away from a
"saving" mentality into "paying MYSELF" mentality*. Get
in the habit of paying yourself first. You've worked too
hard for it to give it all away. The only thing worse than
that is to give it all away before you even have it in hand.
If you're going to do that, go ahead and set up a direct
DEPOSIT to the biller you are obviously working for.

Let me add to this by saying *there is NO investment that
pays residual and reoccurring dividends like investing in
yourself*. Paying yourself is INVESTING in yourself. Way
too often did I witness paycheck to paycheck living and
its as bad as it sounds when it is your paycheck we are
talking about. I know because I lived it for a long time.
The Vienna-fried rice story is an authentic one. I am not
sure I could have made that up if I tried.

Surprisingly there are narratives that lend themselves to
the thought that you can not save due to bills and other

OBLIGATIONS. Stop it. The biller and other obligations often tend to be mostly of our own creation. They exist for all of us - tough. Now you have an opportunity to be able to CLEAR your bills a month in advance if you wanted. Now that you know to pay and invest in yourself first; what does that look like?

You should have your Cash Flow Sheet in hand. Take a look through it and find the one thing that you PAID for that is least valuable to you. Using myself as an example, the first things I notice are the Coffee Shop and Album PURCHASES totaling about $23 (P.s. Get in the habit of calculating your money down to the penny).

Let's say we made coffee in that nice coffee maker we have at home for one day and did not go to the coffee shop. Let's say that we stream our favorite album instead of the full purchase one time.

Do NOT let that wealth sit. Put it into your INVESTMENT account immediately. The quicker it goes in the quicker you wealth is allowed to start working to build more wealth. That's enough about me. Let me show you the "why".

From making our coffee and streaming music instead of purchasing, we have created SPACE for that $23 to work in our lives. This is a secret used by many of the wealthy names I have come across in studying their lives. Transfer those FUNDS into a high-yield savings account such as a Money Market Account (MMA) or CD. For this example we will use 'CD'. Using the following 3-Step process you will plant the seed of wealth in your life. I call it a 3-Step process, but it's truly 4 steps as the first thing you do is set a goal and reverse engineer. I'll show you what I mean.

If I gave you the strategy of a Fortune 100 company that that reports over $20B in annual revenue per year, would you use it?

I'm assuming you would as I'm about to hand you the key to wealth building.

Create your S.M.A.R.T. GOAL for the future, then reverse engineer it into the now (today). Smart goals are tasks that are Specific, Measurable, Achievable, Results-focused, and Time-bound. (**Hint**: you can apply smart goals to anything you want to achieve in a future date and time.)

Example: I want to buy those $1300 black Balmain biker jeans for my birthday 2016.

Questions to ask about your goal.
Is is S.M.A.R.T. (Specific? Measurable? Achievable? Results-focused? Time-bound?)

Yes - black Balmain biker jeans is specific.
Yes - $1300 is measurable.
Yes - a purchase is achievable.
Yes - owning the jeans is the result I desire.

Yes - owning them by my birthday in 2016 is time-bound.

Are you with me so far? Now we have our smart goal, our next step is to reverse engineer it. *This simply means breaking the larger goal down into smaller actionable steps that I can begin today or in the near future.* The first think I like to do here when I teach this method to my sales team is to understand the time and how frequent can you impact it. How many months are between today and my deadline in 2016? Ok, now divide the cost of the goal by the number of months in between. For this example, it's 11 months. ($1300 ÷ 11 = $118.18) This tells me that in order for me to have enough cash to purchase those jeans by my birthday, I need to put away $118.18/month for 11 months.

The greatest thing about this is that you can apply it to anything you can thing of from sales goals to wedding dresses! Another hint here is that I would recommend putting that $118.18 into a high-eliding savings account so that it works for you and grows wealth while you wait. With that, lets get back to our 3-Step Investment plan.

Keep It RIL (when investing)!

Step 1 - **RESEARCH**. Search for high-yielding savings accounts. I have learned that *online banks do not have the overhead cost of brick and mortar locations and thus can offer you higher interest rates*. A great place to stat your research is www.bankrate.com. Its a one stop shop for the best interest rates on saving and money market accounts. Another top site for rates is www.ingdirect.com. Find one that best works for you.

Hint: Online banks will offer you higher interest rates due to them not having to fund brick and mortar institutions.

Step 2 - **INVEST**. Understand, as we have discussed before, that investing comes with the inherent expectation of dividends. *Stop waiting to spend your money from the hard work you put in and begin waiting for your money to create more wealth for you.* This makes me think of 401k plans often offered by employers. If you own your own business, look into the various IRA's available. They function as a similar savings vehicle with arguably better benefits minus the company match benefit of the 401k. You'll notice that they have a cap on the amount you can put into an IRA. That's usually a good sign that you're putting your money in the right place. The reason they do this is because of money's earning potential via gaining interest. You'll see interest rates coming up in a few pages.

If you are a part of an organization that offers the benefit of a 401k, invest in it. Seriously. There is usually a company match for every dollar you put in. That's free money! Take advantage. My thoughts on the 401k are that you should increase your deposit amount to as much

as you can without creating a hardship for yourself.
DO NOT TOUCH YOUR 401K FUNDS barring anything
other than a dire financial emergency. When you
withdraw from your 401k account it acts as taxable
income which with come in the form of TWO tax
penalties. One is the fees when you withdraw the funds
and the other is when you do your taxes and report the
additional income that wasn't taxed. Uncle Sam will want
his up front. I've gone through this and owed over $7000
in taxes as a result.

Step 3 - **LOOK AWAY**. Ever heard the saying about
watching water boil? The essence is that our perception
of time slows to a painful pace as we watch over the pot
awaiting the water to boil. This concept is very real when
you watch your investments. Note that your dividends (in
most cases) will be paid out in percentages on a monthly
basis. For this I advise you to schedule your wealth check
for 1 day a month. Preferably the last day of the month
when the dividends are deposited.

Take a look at how interest works below.

Today the national average interest rate on a basic savings account is .06% according to money.cnn.com. The interest rates available are up to 1.50% Annual Percent Yield (APY).

The math on that works like this. $23 in a 1.5% APY account for 12 months will become $35.43 (creating roughly $0.43) when you add only $1 a month for 12 months.

Better Math: $230 in a 1.5% APY account for 12 months will become $245.56 (creating roughly $3.56) when you add only $1 a month for 12 months.

Last one: $2300 in a 1.5% APY account for 12 months will become $2346.82 (creating roughly $34.82) when you add only $1 a month for 12 months. This is why you want a MILLION dollars in the bank.

I tell you to LOOK AWAY because when we see funds, we are tempted to put our hands on it because of the millions of ads we have seen telling us to buy the millions of things we don't need. Warren Buffet says that people who buy a bunch of things they don't need are the same people that you'll find selling a bunch of things they don't need, but at a loss.

For those of you like me, with spending habits, we have to create tricks to aid us in our wealth building. For you guys, here are a few that I personally have used to increase my rainy day fund by $5000 in this year alone.

As a husband, a father, and a son, I have become highly sensitive to the RELATIONSHIP that my girls have with money. In the beginning I was terrified. That was until I identified the fact that it is the perfect position to alter each of their DESTINIES and help them create a better future for themselves. This book is for Michelle, Kari, Zoey, and my Mom. The plan is to inspire each of you to embrace the challenge of owning your own in this world regardless of your partnerships with others. I hope you read this and SHARE it with your own mothers, daughters, sisters, and friends. This book precedes a course on finance for girls. Take the time to go the the Lorenzoleads™ page on Facebook to CONNECT with me. You may have a question that another is hesitant to ask but need the answer nonetheless. We are on a mission to build something incredibly powerful and to be a part of it, **A GIRL'S GOTTA HAVE HER OWN MONEY**.

Thank you all for helping me change my part of the world and inspire others to do the same. Remember, you have every tool you need to be extraordinary in this world. You are pretty. You are powerful. You are Profitable. Now go be great!

Lorenzo

Lorenzo McNulty is an outstanding husband, brilliant father of three, and a veteran of the United States Marine Corps. As CEO and founder of McNulty Manor LLC, a strategic leadership development company located in Charlotte, NC., he continues to excel in direct and indirect sales and sales leadership across the entire East coast. After an Honorable Discharge from the Marine Corps in 2005, he discovered that his leadership skills from "The Corps" translated into a phenomenal career within corporate America and found himself delivering that Marine level of leadership to two of the largest Fortune 100 telecommunications companies in America for the last 10 years. He divides his strategic leadership into the three distinct categories of Family, Finance, and Business and shows you how to be the Chief Executive Officer (CEO) of each. He has been called a life coach, however he prefers the term Promotion Expert as he often expresses that his purpose is to help you identify yours.. and then teach you to *walk in wealth*.

Connect with Lorenzo:
www.lorenzoleads.com
Linkedin: Lorenzo McNulty
Twitter: @Lorenzoleads
Periscope: @Lorenzoleads
Instagram: @Lorenzoleads

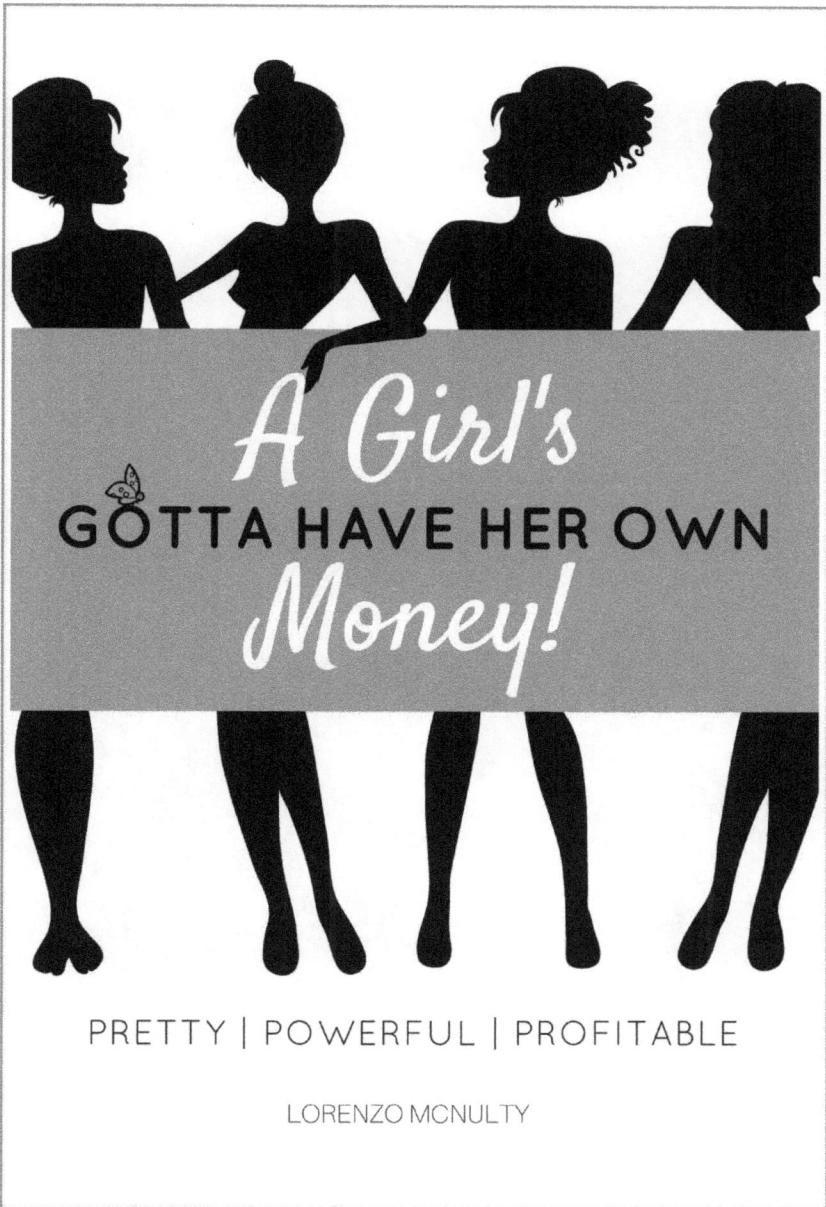

A Girl's GOTTA HAVE HER OWN Money!

PRETTY | POWERFUL | PROFITABLE

LORENZO MCNULTY

A Girl's Gotta Have Her Own Money

www.ingramcontent.com/pod-product-compliance
Lightning Source LLC
Chambersburg PA
CBHW030154070426
42447CB00032B/1176